the bottled up feelings

-K. Kanda

Published by: Hemingway Publishers
Cover designed by: K. Kanda
ISBN: 978-1-967927-77-7, printed in the United States

i started to write down the words that
did not reach their ears.
at least, i hope the world is not blind.

contents

a dream

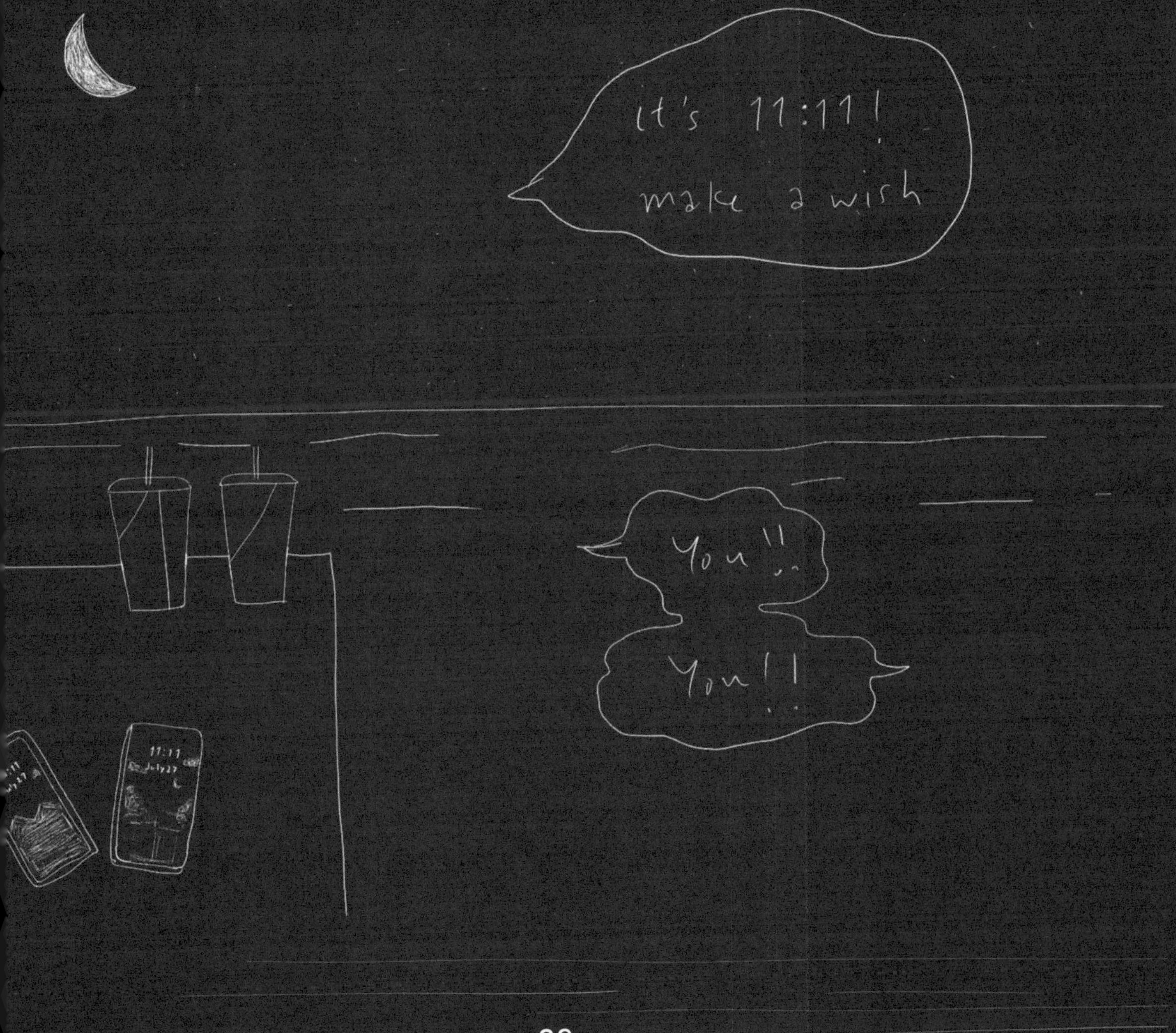
it's 11:11!
make a wish
You!!
You!!

a year ago
i was struggling to keep swimming
in the ocean
of my emotions,
dreams, and
realities

a home
in which i spent more than 20 years of my life
watching it as i was leaving
saying to myself

"i'd take that little girl to different places now"

even though i knew
i wouldn't be able to call
any of them
'home'
but somehow
it would still be okay
but i never knew
i'd find my home
in somebody's smile

i'm a fool to wish upon the stars
to want to see you again
and then tell them
you're more magical and prettier
than them

♥ 🗨 ➤   🔖

liked by **nobody** and **others**

rollingcaterpillar

the best thing you told me was
"you're the reason i wake up happy these
days" ..and i feel the same :)

all of the places that we have been to
your eyes looked up for the magic that
the universe holds for you
while i just looked at you

you said "be on the same page",
if i'm not,
you will claim to write your words
on my book.

and i,
i'd never dare to erase them ever.

if i get lost in the words,
promise me
that you'll pull,
and bring me back to
where we were before,
and i promise,
i'll follow each and every letter
that you'll engrave
through your heart.

let's play with poetries,
and build chapters,
but if i take my turn to write,
i only hope
you to read
and see through my eyes.

i just want us
to keep taking steps together
towards new pages
and never finish off.

i'm proud to see
the ocean in you
even the high tides of it
may wash me away

you can blow me away
like i'm your perfect wish

and i'll carry myself away
for it all along

as i was made for it

You'll be forever my moon person

there's no going back to the stars completely

SEE THE MOON!

YOO!

your eyes

they know the way to my heart
and they don't even know about it

in this universe
we're made out of stardust
and when we align
all of the constellations gather up too
to comprehend all the magic and spells
we are capable to cast

you are exactly
all of those dreams
my heart
used to wish for

and if i tell you
i don't remember
how you look like
it's because
you feel like a dream
to me

i saw the miracles going inside you
the day i saw your eyes
it felt like
the beginning of an eclipse
and when you close your eyes
a comet strike all over my small town

what is love
i'm not sure of it
but i wonder what is it like
when i realize
your smile is the one
i want to see for the rest of my life

it's the solace that i feel
when i see your face
when i'm on the verge of crying

it's the concern that i perceive
when you'd show me your fingertips
like a child
saying that they hurt
playing four strums on your guitar
and i'd just rub them taking my heart out
cheering you up, saying,
"you're doing great!"

it's my readiness
to make myself a fool
to see you smile and laugh

it's the sadness that i drown in
when you roll your eyes away from me

it's like an elixir to my soul
when your eyes look for me
and i see
i'm the one
to make you smile

what is love
we'll never be sure of it
but i know that
i'm even ready to
live only with all of these
realizations
for my whole life

you are the purest formation of
soul wrapped by clouds and stars
the thought of touching you
scares me that
i may taint the purity

little things matter to me.

when you hit me up in morning
with just two-letter text "yo",

when i'm all drained out,
you come along with a sweet package
of smile,
and i ask "what do you want?",
then you say nothing,
but just point your finger at me,

when you ask all those random questions
and i answer somehow.
you'd say with contentment
"this is exactly what i wanted to hear",

when your phone rings
you don't even bother to check it
and then say
"it doesn't matter,
 because you're here with me",

the tiny silly opinions,
a short call after a whole exhausting day,
a text "i'm home".

all these little things,
they matter.

it feels
good to
have
someone

when you
reach your place
and tell me
"i'm home"

i say
"yes, you are."

- mine

i love the way how you get
excited about little things
and i can spend every life
in the multiverse just watching that

in the night sky,
your soul shines
brighter than the stars
and you ask me
why am i having my eyes
on you?

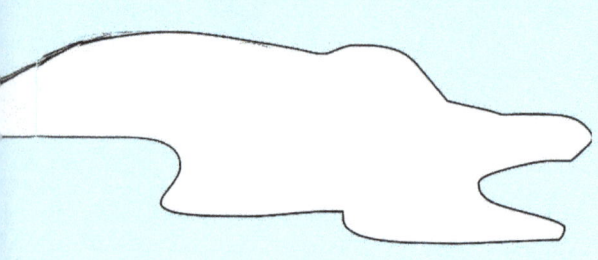

in this life,
we choose to play our roles.
we can build a castle or
cast a movie.
you just be whoever
you want to be.
i'd just want to be with you.

i know
i'm a little obsessed with you
and i admit that

my heart tells me
that i'm at a safe place
when i can listen
your heart beating
next to mine

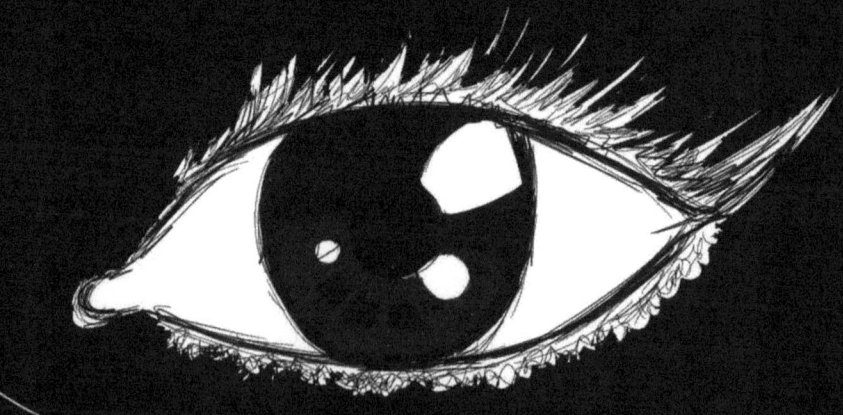

Your eyes hold the spark of
a million stars

your eyes
are the most beautiful place
where i can live

i always want to be there for you.
good or bad,
through thick and thin.

i want to hold your hand,
even if i have to aspire through hell.

i want to see you shine.
i want to see that fire in your eyes.
you know,
you can put that damn sun down
and stars fade out
with your spark.

i just want to be there
for you, and with you
when you bloom flowers all over yourself
and say with a smile
"look! i made it".

the innocence
that your soul holds
even angels would fall
for that

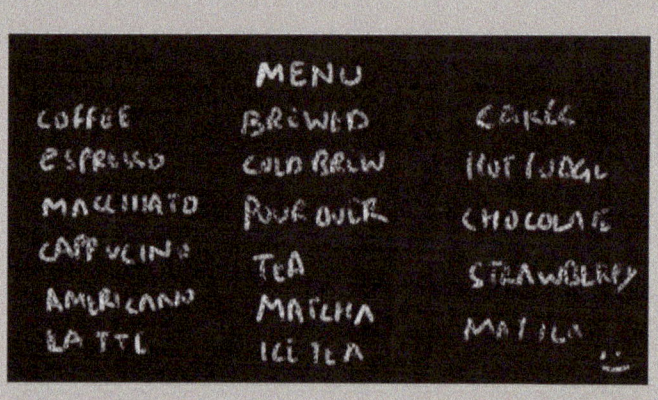

i ask you about your
plans and
wish to be a part of
them

you have not been my habit
you have been my ritual

wanna show you off
like a trophy
but gotta keep you safe
like a treasure

the way you hold my hand
feels like
you're gonna call out stars
to sing my name

let me just taste the heaven
that you hold in you
i've been in hell for years
let me build a home at the place
from where you see stars
and i'll catch the shooting stars
for you with my bare hands

i wish you to call me by a name
that you'd choose only for me

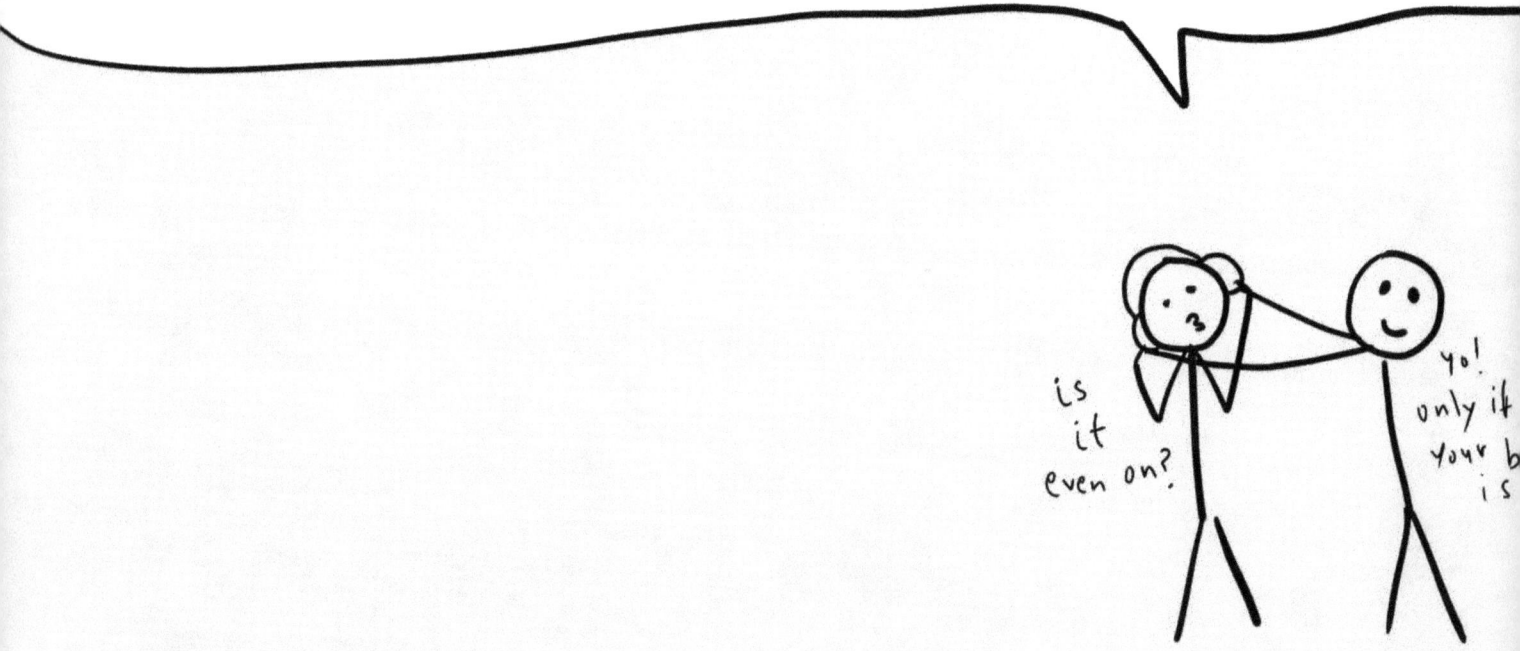

You're gonna get everything in your life that you yearn for...
a note for you

a crack
in it

you feel way too magical
to be standing in front of me

i'm afraid if i touch your face
my fingers might disappear into air

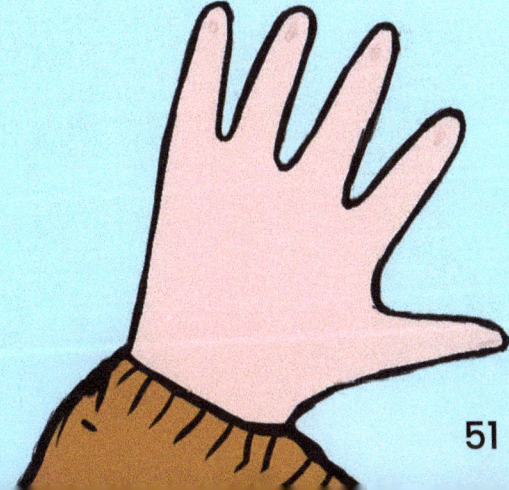
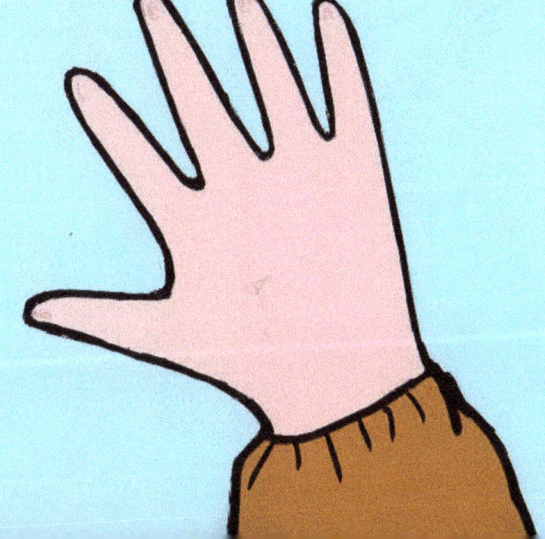

i'd try my best
not to look
into those eyes
because i know
they'd drag me deep down

i'll fall and fall
and i'll drown in them
there's no doubt i won't love it
but i know
there isn't coming back

how beautiful is it
to have someone
yet it's lonely

you are the sun
i revolve around in orbit
your gravitational force is cruel
that i never get to touch
but somewhat 2.36 million seconds
in a month
being around you
i cut myself in half and more
then i disappear
and then i strive to be whole
but i'm still little-known to you

i feel like
i'm a part of the leaves
that drop down dead
on the ground
during autumn

you look at it
you smile and
say
"isn't it beautiful?"

i felt the closest to you,
and now
a whole universe
away

i think
i've been more easy
in chaos,
comfort has always
got me panicked
that as there's something
to lose.

i started loving you with no expectations
because i wasn't ready for another heartbreak.
i knew,
i would give you my all
as i fall into your innocence.

the day when you got off the bus
and waited for me at the bus stop
it got me surprised that
you'd do this for me?

'waiting'

one day,
you called me on my phone twice
just to let me know,
saying,
"i'm here, okay?"

then another day,
you just held my hand.

another day,
you put your head on my shoulder.

days passed and then again,
another day,
you said,

"i guess, this is it! i want to be with you.
 even if there's nobody else around, i'd be
 happy just being with you."

how can i love you without any expectations?
at least that i expected was that
you'll stay.

it doesn't matter what i feel
maybe i was just born to love
and built to lose in it

how am i supposed to feel
if i feel replaced in it
i'll turn the lights off
put myself to sleep

and i'd try my best not to shed
another tear this time
because i know
it's nobody's fault
maybe this is just how it is

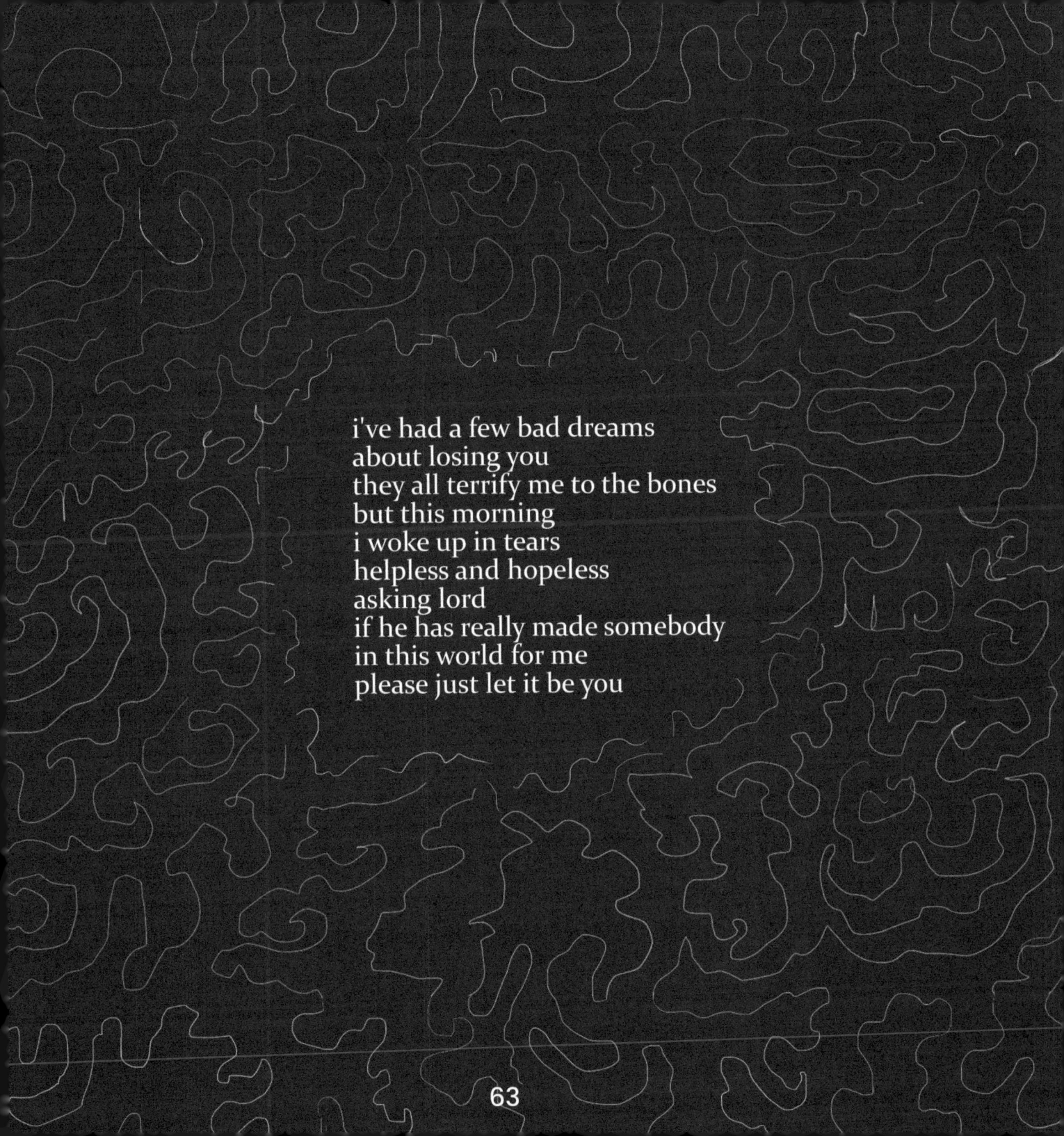

i've had a few bad dreams
about losing you
they all terrify me to the bones
but this morning
i woke up in tears
helpless and hopeless
asking lord
if he has really made somebody
in this world for me
please just let it be you

and i cried like rain
as its water drips down
on window pane
the trickling sound of it
in the middle of the night
never bothered you to
open your eyes again

now that i feel
i don't fit here anymore in this world
i'm still trying to validate my feelings
through the storms

the transition from day to night
sometimes feels as quick as a snap
other times
it feels like forever
as i am getting dragged around
every second with the strike of a clock

what i feel
i hope that's not a part of the sins or
the religion
where they burn the witches on a stake or
nail them to the wall
i'm trying to admire every part of myself
hoping my soul to be safe
when i leave this world

there's no way
i can keep you forever.
i've always loved
the stars, moon, jellyfishes and birds.

embracing them has always felt
like a dream to me,
like an idea,
i can't even put my hands upon them.

if i choose to be vulnerable around you
please don't let it be a mistake

console me with your plausible words
as i'm not aware of them
but all i want is you
to open your arms for me
so i can sink into them
so i can bury my lonely heart into your chest
it hurts to see
that my silence doesn't bother you at all
i may be your amusement only
when i make nice jokes
still with every move i make
i hope you'd want to see me
so i wave from the stage in my innocence
and when the curtains close
i look for you if you have come
to the backstage
to meet

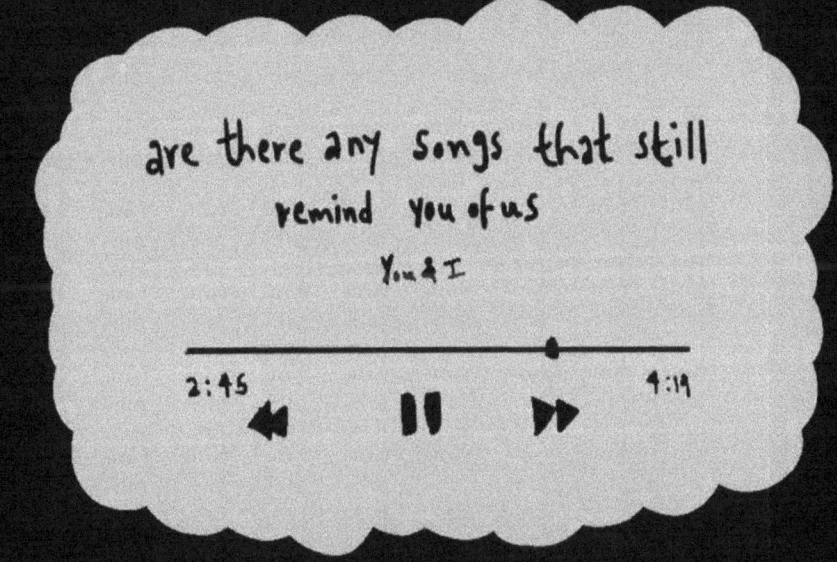

if there comes a day
when my eyes won't find their way
back to you,
way back to home,
they will look for you everywhere
but would sink down every time
with the thought of you.

all i'd do,
play songs to relate,
play movies to picture out the days.
maybe i'd go to the places
where i felt the embrace,
and when i'll come back,
maybe i'd tell myself that
i knew this wasn't just meant to be.
i didn't have enough time,
so i tried my best.

then i'd write about you,
because all of these things will bring me
closer to you.
then maybe i'd go back to sleep
and repeat again.

it's funny
how every person feels
a single emotion differently

i'd feel everything in extremes
and you'd feel nothing at all

i think i'm always gonna choose
the most dangerous ways to get my heart broken
because i've never learnt doing anything
without giving my all

i'd go deep down
i'd drown
i'd feel in extremes
so i'd break in extremes
and the process of fixing myself back again
feels chaotic and endless

i shatter
i fall apart
the pieces of mine maybe will never be found
because it's like an explosion at first
but later
it slowly creeps down my soul
with some obnoxious voices echoing in my mind

and the cycle of it
is exhausting
how long can i stay in it
how long can i live with it
when it keeps on repeating
and the only place that gives me solace is
where there is no hope at all

i'm stuck between

"should i do this or should i not?"
"should i say this or should i not?"

"did i say too much
or did i say nothing at all that was meant
to be said?"

"i hope it won't seem like i'm possesive."
"oh, i hope it won't seem like i don't
care at all."

"if i say i want to see you.
i want to meet you.
i hope i'm not being clingy
or if i just wait, and do nothing,
i hope that won't make me look aloof and
unconcerned."

"maybe i should take this for you
but wait,
what if it looks like i'm too obsessive"

"what if i tell you that i miss you?
i hope it won't sound so desperate but
what if i play it cool and our memories
from your head fade away."

i'm always stuck in 'in-betweens'
and my thoughts are oscillating
as they are on a seesaw.

i crave to be understood.
i crave for an emotional connection.
i yearn for that excitement that i used to feel in your voice,
telling me about your day.
you'd say,

"i wanna save my energy, just so i can talk to you.
 i don't wanna feel already drained out when i'm with you."

i long for those eyes
that would look just for me
when the day is over.

it feels sad not to be the one
that i was to you before.
so, i put myself through an intensive investigation.
i lock myself up in my room
to interrogate,
'why and where did it go wrong'.
a thousand of questions,
doubting every single thing that i had done and still do,
and it gets really ugly
when i don't trust myself to be accountable
for my own emotions anymore.

i don't know if it even makes sense,
i just don't understand what's my fault
to be liable for this hurt.
all i wanted was just
to be on that one same page,
but my longings have ripped out
all of the pages in mourn.

we are not on the same page anymore
it's not even the same book

if somebody cares
about you
but doesn't care
about your feelings

i'm sorry
that's not love

i guess we are all
afraid to be just a phase
in that someone's life

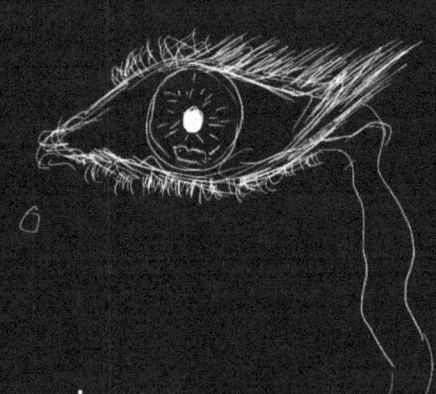

when i'm with you
i see every possibility coming to me.

a dream dreamt,
casting spells.
like the moon is ready to embrace me
and the stars are ready to take me to the beach,
but when you're gone,
it all disappears
as it was just a world
that i built myself in the corners of my head,
and then a salt river passes down in my room
making me forget how to breathe,
then the consciousness
brings me down to my knees.

it asks me to take a step back,
but it all feels like
i'm just a mouse in a cage,
running on the wheel,
propelling it to move forward
but nothing seems to be working out,
it all just repeats.

i think
we had been closer
or maybe i was just feeding
myself with imagination
to take a breath
out of reality

i'll still be broken,
and you're going to build up
a house with the pieces of mine

and you'll still dare
to call it a home

how am i supposed to like
those trickster tornadoes
that have given me
nightmares of taking
my home away

i wish we didn't have this ego.
i don't even know if it's an ego or what,
but i halt to take my steps towards you.
i think a million times.
i believe even 5-year-olds
can keep friendships alive better,
and love deeper than us.

i could not tolerate the reality,
and perhaps that is why i bled on you.

sometimes i feel it'd be better
if the existence of mine disappears
into thin air
as an idea of desired love.

i keep on asking the ocean, moon, stars
for what my heart pines for,
like they do have ears
to listen to my nonsense,
as if they are meant to do that.

resentment, desertedness, incapacitation
are the feelings that shouldn't be in circles
and then again,
there it goes,
that feeling
that maybe you were never meant
to be born here
in this world.

meeting you feels as going
on a war with myself now.
i look at you,
i crave to take you into my arms forever.
i just want to set my eyes upon on you
because i love the way how your smile
feels like home to me.

it's hard to resist
the comfort that i feel
when i'm around you,
this safety is all
i'd been looking for my entire life.

i'd say 'hi'
when i see you,
but then it'd be a death for me
to say 'goodbye' to you
when you leave.

then i remind myself,
i need to let you go,
but it doesn't matter either,
because i know,
every time,
i'm gonna surrender in this war.

why don't you ask
for help?

i guess, i'm too
vulnerable for that

i just wish
you'd make me sit
beside you
and ask me
how i really feel
on the inside

-the real talk

sometimes i'd start my sentences
with '..and'
to vaguely depict that
just in case if you capture,
i've got a lot to say and tell
but i'll put that up in
a bottomline for you
so it won't bore you

-i hope you are interested to know

i should have taken
the emergency exit
when they set my house
on fire
but i was too busy admiring
the flames

i wanna tell you that
'i miss you
and wish to hear the
same

you may not want to cross the sea
of cold tyranny anymore to get to me
but look
how all my resentments melt away
even when i wait at the shore
with my hope all alone by merely
imagining your face

how can i stop loving you
when i breathe every day
with the thoughts of you?

the thought of
'you and i'.

as our friendship falls apart,
as i see you every time,
you are one more inch away
from my heart.

i still wish to say
what we have become now
is a different story.
a story,
that may not meant
to be happy in this universe
but in another somehow.

breakdown

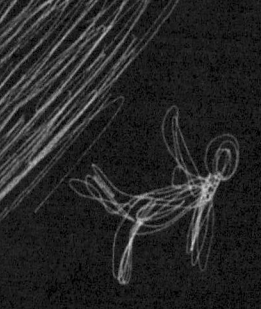

there's something about grief
that pulls you in
and you start to feel
okay to be there in it.

it's like you're falling into
a black hole.
you'd bleed
and would be torn apart,
and you know,
the thought of getting out of it
would feel fictitious forever,
and the thought of spending
rest of your life in it
would be a torture,
and the next thing
you know,
you're falling down
deeper and deeper in it
until it shatters you down.

freefall

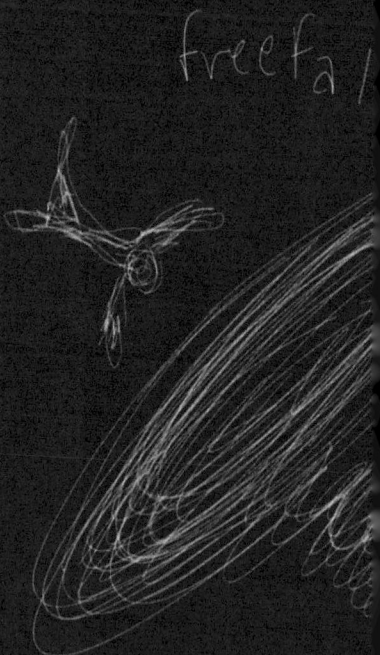

love is a dangerous
thing, it will sell
you out and the one
in front of you
won't even feel a thing

i was just an open wound

when i bleeded out

it just got you scared

and run away

you put your arms around my shoulders
as they belong to them
slow danced as it's not the end of the year but
the end of this whole world
clinged to me
as our hearts beat in the same chest
and when i started to believe that
it's not a dream
you threw me away
like i was just clinging to your neck
like an old necklace
that doesn't go with new trends

what good my arms are
for if they can't hold you

it's better to break them

if they can't have you

i wish i can tell you
how lonely i am without you
in some beautiful way
so that you'd come back

i see
i walk through
the same roads, same places every day
and the flashbacks
they never stop to chase me down

i see us
the way it was
it feels like
it was just a dream
and now i'm stumbling on these roads again
all alone by myself
living in delusions that i'll see you again

if i'm being honest
i don't feel like going to the place
they call 'home'
because once
i called you mine

i still haven't pulled up the curtains
in my room
because the open windows remind me
of you leaving
and it sinks my heart down in this pain
how will i ever be capable to let you go
this is not fair to me

you were a friend with whom
i could talk with no words.
fun?
i couldn't even take my smile off
my face every morning
from the moment
i'd open my eyes.

3rd of february,
you left.
you never came back,
and neither did my smile.

the places that felt like home to me
now make me feel more lonely

you don't need me
and that's obvious.

i remember when i got so scared
of my anxious thoughts about losing you,
you held me and said
"there's no way i am leaving you."
and i almost cried saying
"i need you. you don't need me, i know,
  ..but i need you."
and you somehow said it as well
"i need you too."

almost everything has changed
we have been so distant,
disconnected.
i guess we both are trying
to fill up the invisible space
between us.
i can see,
you just want to fill up those gaps
but i am still in a need to fix up all these cracks,
and trust me,
it's exhausting.

i don't really blame you,
i know there's no one to blame,
you still care,
but i know,
you'd never need me like i need you.,
you have your friends,
they are nice.
you have a new life.

for me
it's still 2 am
and i'm sitting on the pavement
behind a closed mall,
where i said to you

"i need you."

i don't know
if it's the emptiness
hollowing my chest
or the loneliness
heaving my heart

i heard the birds chirp
sitting on the branches
they were telling each other
they don't want to talk to me
while i just stood there
until they flew down to say
the same to my face

what is loneliness?

it's just a word
but i feel it to the depths.

it creeps upon me like
ivy growing
on an abandoned house.

the cracks
that i have received
now feels like
a structural damage to me.
i've been filling them up
with every chemical that
i can barely afford to get.
even though,
i am aware of the fact that
in actual what they need
is something else.

it splatters onto my bones,
eats me down,
inch by inch,
it only grows
just to erase me out.

for you,
it's just a word.

for me,
it's a sad song
that plays every day on repeat.

what is loneliness?

it is
when i wake up in the morning
and all i can think about is that
you're not here anymore.

i check my phone to see your name in it,
instead i scroll down to find it.

i wait for you to reply,
i wait for you to call,
it's getting an everyday thing,
and i recall,
how i'd wait to hear from you,
about how your day was,
and now i just keep on checking the clock
and then my phone.

on my way to work,
i just see the flashbacks of us
being together at the places that i pass,
and when i come back,
i see there's no one
to listen
how my day was.
i sleep every night with hope,
probably you'd call and talk to me
next day, or next week, or next month,
and then this nightmare
will finally be over.

i surrendered myself to love
instead it devoured me

i thought that we were
inseparable and now we
are living in our own
separate worlds

is it okay to expect from a friend?
they say it's not healthy at all to expect
anything from anyone.
even trees deny to hold the leaves every fall.
i knock on your door today, then tomorrow,
just to hear you answer 'no'.
silly me! i still save my saturdays
telling other people "i have plans",
then i wait for you and watch you go.

please, don't push me away again.
it's another day for me of trying.
isn't it pathetic?
i never change,
i never grow.
instead i play cool,
as if i'm not affected,
i'm not hurt at all.
how would you notice my tears
when you close your eyes from me?
how can you say one thing to me today,
then blame it on the nature of the weather tomorrow?

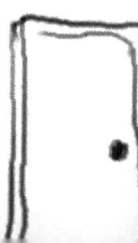

there are times when i wonder
how long my life would be
i'm tired of the yearnings and pining

here i'm again
feeling left out
looking for the arms that held me once
and now refuse
to hold me in there anymore

lost
shattered
deranged
losing my serenity as it'd never come back
there will be just tears coming out in the rain

i keep on thinking where i went wrong
then the death crosses my mind
i wait for it to arrive
as i see no end of this sorrow either

i cried oceans to sleep
last night
repeating to myself

i hate you
i hate you
i hate you

indeed we both know the truth

what hurts is to know that
you're my kryptonite.

you used to claim that
i'm yours and said,

"don't you worry! there can't be anybody
who would ever take me away from you.
i'll be here, always by your side."

you used to say that you just need to see me
and you'll be okay.
you gave your ears to listen to my silence
and would just be there for me
with the sun and the moon
in your hands
when even a single word was too heavy
for me to spill out.

what hurts,
it's to realize the fact
that priorities are an option too.
i spent my
every single day with you last year,
and now this year,
i've barely seen you.

what hurts,
it's to see that
other people are now closer to you
and most of the times,
our conversations go
into awkward silences.

what hurts,
it's that
i sit by my phone now
waiting for you to call,
then i turn it off
to turn down the expectations
and the anticipations of disappointments.

what hurts
is that i know,
you're my kryptonite,
and i know,
i'd learn to smile with it.

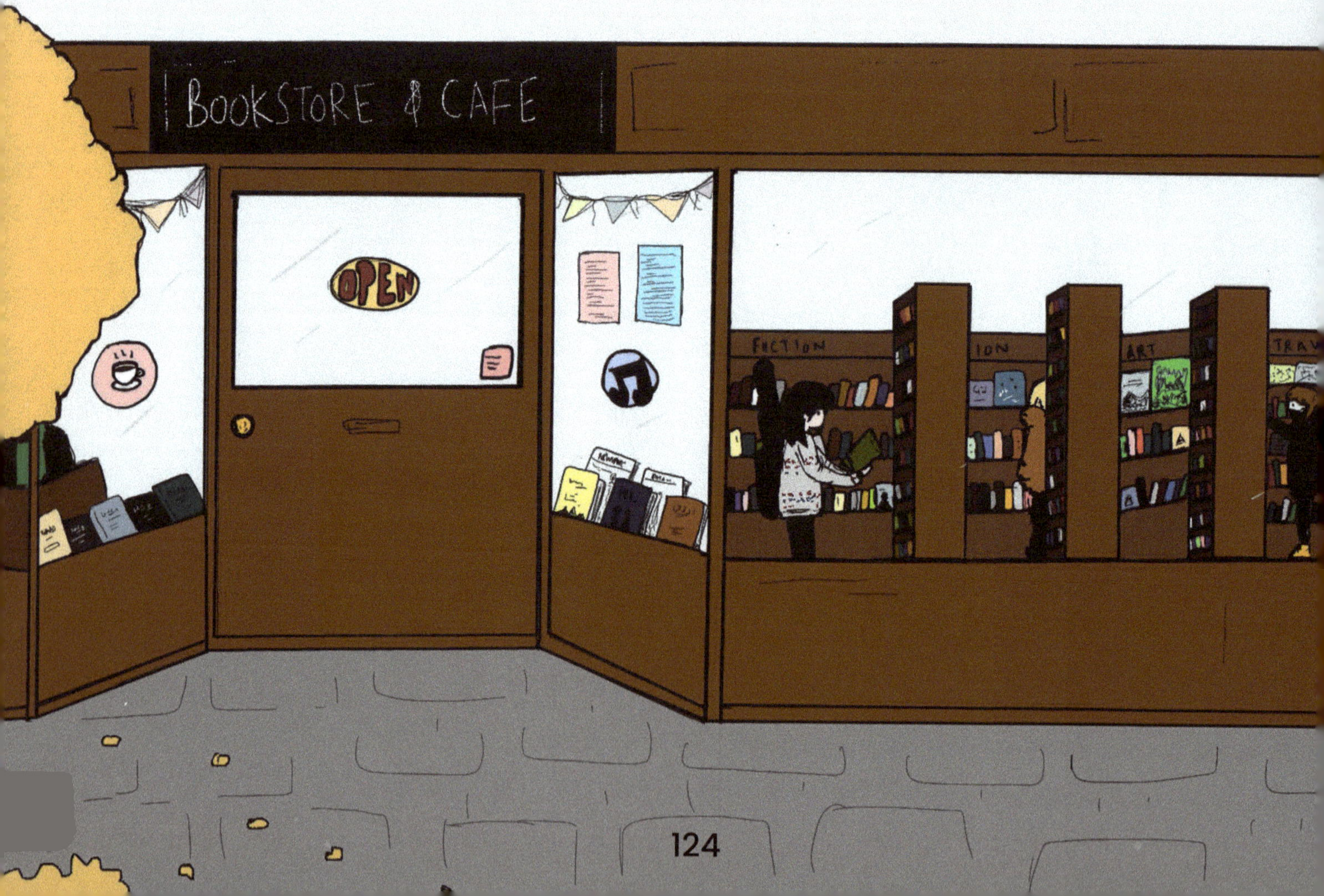
BOOKSTORE & CAFE
OPEN
FICTION
ART

it's so ironic that
you don't wanna know me anymore
when once you said
you wanna know me the most

my heart has never been taken
seriously,
perhaps the body that carries it
isn't right

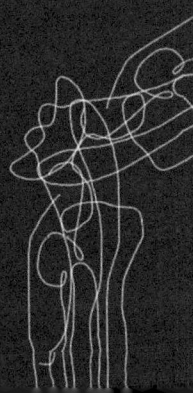

sunflowers,
why don't you look at me?
i may not be your sun
but why can't you see,
i bring the light for you
burning myself across the creek.

i doubt it.
i quench myself,
and see
if i burnt myself right.
i guess,
i have figured it out.
i'll light myself up better this time.
if i strike the match really slow and
ignite the flames through my chest first,
i won't be in grief this time
that you didn't look at me.

let me try again.
this time,
from the top of my head.
so that i won't hold any resentments.
so this time,
will you talk to me?

i can't hear you.
that's okay.
this time,
i'll start the burning from my ears.
so i won't die to hear your sound,
the words i don't get to hear.

but why won't you still look at me?
lord knows how many times
i'd try different ways to burn myself up.
i'd rather be in ashes,
if i can't be the sun to you.

it's
12 am
12:11 am
12:20 am
12:35 am
12:48 am

...
it's my birthday
and it's funny
i'm still waiting
for your call

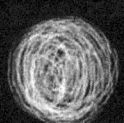

i packed my bag and left the house
so that i won't have to answer the demons
that knock at my door around 2 am

hiding myself in a hood
hoping no ghost would follow me
but wishing for an angel to save me

roaming the whole town
running and escaping
playing all the possible manipulative games
with my own brain

oh a sudden heart attack
the devil has his eyes on me
he is trying to chase me down in the street

i come back running to my room
sit on the floor
on my knees
praying the spirits for an angel to keep

it just creeps me out
how time changes everything.
it fades away the past,
it builds up memories,
it heals the broken,
but it also brings the apocalypse.

i'm scared,
it will do everything for you,
in your favor,
and you will barely remember
how we used to be,
but it may not do anything for me.
i guess, i'll still be at the same place.

it's a feeling,
it's a phase,
it's all simple to say.
indeed, i struggle to breathe
in the fire you set to my home
and the entire world sounds
like an endless scream to me.

how can i ask for help?
they will call me insane and weird.

i know, i'm boring
and no fun,
but i can use a set of arms
around my chest
as an armour for my heart,
but i'm afraid to say that
it's too late to save
what's already drowned
and dead.

i sink into these walls,
telling them how i feel.
i don't want to sound
despairing,
because they will run away.
but i sort of wait for things,
and life,
to end in some way.

in some way,
that when i wake up every morning,
i won't say to myself anymore,
"what's the point of everything?"

i was running around
looking for something
that wasn't even in my
consciousness,
and when i saw you,
i halted.
i took a sigh of relief, and
said to myself,
"this is it. i don't have to
run anymore."

how small do i look?
like the size of your fingernail that
you cut right away when it feels heavy
on your skin?

it's ironic,
you just walk around,
pass by, and walk away,
as i was never born.
and i never let go,
as a ghost,
i mourn and whine.

blood is red in color,
even the dead knows.
those words can be stifling,
that say,

"it's not the same."
"you've been too desperate."

all of this is enough to rip off
the chest of the one
who longs to see the golden gaze
of someone's eyes.
you can say the things that you yearn
to hear to console yourself,
and then to stop the shaking,
pat on your own heart.

i'm still too small, i guess.
my jaw aches to find you
not looking at me,
not even for once.
i'm looking to buy
some nice hooks
everyday
to stretch my cheeks
to the bones.

if i disappear,
would you care to search
if i'm breathing?
i think my death would be
in silence,
in an empty room.
maybe
it would be suspicious,
like a murder.
when i won't answer my phone
for days,
the force will break in
and find out that
i was stabbed multiple times
by my own demons,
but there will be no clue
that i was trying to dance with
them during the whole time.

i smiled and entertained
to be liked
but i guess
i didn't perform good enough
at that as well

i felt
i was just a substitute
as your thoughts and feelings
replaced with others

there's always something else
or someone else
if it's not me
there would be someone else

that's okay! Bye!

8:36 PM

Bye!

8:39 PM

i'm not the one anymore
who you'd tell about your days
i'm not the one any more

i'm always on the
swing of my emotions
that's why they call it mood swings ?!

H
u're
AYIN?!

a part of me wants to pack my bags
and leave this city,
not because
i'm sick of its busy life.
it's because every spot of it
holds your memories.

then another part of me
always unpacks the suitcase
of all those moments that i had with you.
they lighten up hope in me that
maybe i'd see you
somewhere,
somehow.
so i prefer to say
that i want to stay.

maybe i'll never learn
the art of letting go
so i'll just try to learn
to live with it

maybe i'll make a home
for my loneliness
at least it will have me

they say
'fake it till you make it'
so i'm trying to picture that
nothing happened.
we are still good,
we still talk every day,
we still see each other.
there's nothing like
i'm the only one left in this all
alone,
you're here with me too,
as you always were.

so i'm faking that
i don't miss you anymore too.

sometimes i fake that
i'm happy without you
but in this single war
with a thousand trials
i know
i can't

i carry this void in myself
and wish to end it
taking trips anywhere far from the places,
where they don't remind me the aches of solitude.
when i come back,
i found myself even more hollow
than ever before.
i force myself to smile
because i swear that
i so want to be happy,
but it doesn't seem to be working out.
i cheer myself raising up my voice to talk
but it gets supressed.
i try to speak again,
but i guess,
your name has caught up on my tongue
like a chronic disease.
why nothing excites me anymore ?
i pull myself to talk to strangers.
i wonder, how do they have fun?
could you teach me that too?
teach me how to talk.
teach me how to behave too.
it's embarrassing!
then i long for my own company.

i wished to end the feeling of
loneliness but it ended me

'formal conversations'
'a stranger to a best friend'

was the least i wanted.

i've always looked at you
feeling helpless
because i realize
i'll always adore,
but can never
have you.

'out of my league'
'it's not meant to be',

this is what they say

i keep on reminiscing
how beautiful it was
when you chose to
interlace two worlds in one,
but now it feels like your memory
has washed away.

- you're somebody else

you just made me feel
like
i'm nobody to you

so let it be this time

you were grown enough
to move on,
wise enough to explore
new dimensions.
i was just a child,
simple enough to love you
and mad enough to scream
that i hate you
because you won't even look at me.
then when you're gone,
the silly me
would just wait again as a dog,
sitting on the front porch
looking for you to come back.

i was dying to be your
favorite escape

and i died

MAKE
A SNOW
ANGEL!

i guess i just want
the best parts of my life back
the best connection
the best moments i've ever had
the best places
coffee and book dates
stumbling in streets with you
at 2 am
and then crashing on a park
bench for a while
just to talk and look at the sky
to find shooting stars

everything
when it was all about us
i guess
i just want my best friend back

i know i should let it go
i can't throw my feelings upon you
as you unfold every layer of yourself

and
underneath it
when you find something new
that you don't know how to deal with
i know i should go more easy on you
instead of asking you
to comfort my insecurities

it kinda scares me out
when someone says,

"i'm with you"

because i know
what it takes to stand
next to someone,
close to someone,
or even just to stay...

...and i'm not sure
if i can do that
for someone anymore.

i can't afford to believe it too
that someone would really stand
next to me
because just in case,
if they leave,
the spot next to mine,
it will always be
the cause of my void.

tonight i'm letting you go,
i'm trying to get you out of my mind.
you can't live in there,
you can't be my purpose,
and you can't be the reason
for my existence.
i know,
i'd love you forever
when 'forever' is only a word
that we used before.

and as the way i saw you leaving,
so perfectly,
so flawless,
even then,
i couldn't take my eyes off of you
hoping you'd look back,
and i was crumpled up
just as the piece of paper in my pocket,
the piece on which i wrote only for you.

i can keep on writing,
but i'm going to let you go
even if it takes
specifically that
'forever'.

bloom

i feel that
there are still some good days
left for me to experience with you
so i wish i could fast forward
these ones
that i'm having
right now
and skip to the ones that
take me to you

you bloom daisies
and i grow thorns
how were we supposed
to hold each other

i drowned in you
forgetting i could fly,
broken wings that i had been patching up,
i left them on the table to die.

i ran to get the door
like some 5-year-old kid
when i heard the door bell.
knowing that you would be
on the other side of the door,
i asked you to come in and
i picked up my favorite crayons
to draw a perfect sky together
in the living room.
i dressed myself with daisies in it
and i asked you to color the stars that i drew.
why?
because i saw my moon in you.

i knew you were meant to be in
the floating space.
it made me proud that
you hold the strength to discover the planets and
build a whole new universe of your own,
but you don't know
it hurts to be a much more of an observant.
so hush!
i am a person
digging up the theories, harmonies, and context
of even colors before i paint,
but you, you again,
would build a masterpiece in a second,
before you even set your eyes on the wall.

but how can we leave this mess open
on the table and not talk about it,
pretending it was never there?

i just came back to my little town
after being done waiting and looking
for what i never had.
i glue those daisies on my wings and
patch them up to take a flight.
you had gone miles away
but i keep you here,
in my imagination
and say goodbye to the nights
i spent weeping.

i wish you'd never have to walk
on the roads that i walked on
just to have a glimpse of you at midnights

nobody stays forever,
but for how long
who wants to stay,
that matters.
so as long as the time exists,
i choose to be with you.

i have
crush
on
you

oh!
cut
c

i'm learning
to keep my heart
in the palm of my hands
to offer you my love
but not to break it

it's funny how you'd

just say the things that

i've been feeling

and you don't even know

about it

i don't wanna hurt you
and you can't hurt me anymore
but sometimes i think that
the size of your fingers
are still enough to rip off my chest

but i can take control of the bleedings

someone told me
your brain is designed to keep you safe.
it knows
all the facts,
all the things that are right for you,
but your heart is the one
that gives you trouble.
the one,
that can't be resisted.

so you'd run to get yourself hurt
just to get a glimpse of the sun.
you'd run to take the risk
to get to the moon
and bleed through your chest and eyes.

but your brain is the one
that is going to keep you safe.
it knows all the facts,
all the things
in the whole world
and what's right for you,
but it'd never know
how to make your heart happy.

and i know,
i am not happy.

my overconcerning nature is a crime,
and
my consolation takes years and
thousands of dimes to convince myself
that it's alright

i know nobody stays forever
what do they say is that
everything is temporary
but having you by my side
made me believe that
'temporary' itself
is just a word
which is temporary
you'll be forever a part of me
because i scanned
your fingerprints
with mine

i don't miss you anymore,
and i won't even tell it,
because i'm learning to let you go.

but i still think about you
when i see the moon.
i recall how i'd hit your phone
with a picture of it,
saying "see the moon".

i know i should let it go,
and i'm trying,
but it's getting harder everyday.

as i leave this house and shut the door,
this place always ends up making me say,
"oh! this is where i used to wait for you before".
it's just the same house, same room, same places.
it was about us before,
but now it's only all me.

i know i'm gonna think of you
during the fall because
you love the colors of it.
i know i'm gonna think of you
on the fall of first snow
because we made a silly pact
to be together for it,
as we did for new year's eve.

it's funny,
how you'd just text me right away,
"it's gonna rain! don't forget your raincoat."
when checking out on weather was a big deal
for me back then.

i'm not sad anymore,
and i don't mind
that you chose to leave.
there's not a day that passes
when i don't think about you.
i hope that you're okay,
and wonder what you must be doing?
then somehow
i come back to this fact that
i need to learn
to let you go.

i peer through the window
of my head
just to see
how you bloom everyday

as i see the sun
i wait for my shadow
to meet yours
well, i can't ignore
the past concussion
it still has its hold on me
but i wish
i could choose my skin
or i could choose my skin
or i could take my shape
like water
just so you'd like me

i can't ignore
my past concussion again
i can't unsee the storm
that took my solace away from me
i'd kill it, if i could
i still wonder why you would hide
why would you lie
you've been the lily perched upon
my crown
and you always will be

so i tell myself
you needed a garden to grow
so i'll let you go

i still keep the book
that you gave me
with a polaoird of us in it
and a birthday card that you
once made me.
i take it with me
wherever i go.
i've read half of it,
purposely untouched.
perhaps, i'd never want to
finish it off,
because i'd never want the story
of us to finish off.

my mind never stops
a second to imagine,
what i can teach you the
best is to dream

i let the devil take me,
put me behind the bars.
i let his demons dress me up,
one by one,
they coerced me to put on
the sweatpants of depression,
brainwashed me to wear
the sweatshirt of insecurities,
and on the top of my head,
a hat full of anxieties.
then, he released me out in the world,
asking demons to keep an eye on me.

i said, and i screamed that
i want to take these clothes off,
rip my skin off,
but instead, i let these clothes define me
and forgot who i used to be,
what i used to dream.

the ones i loved,
i made it so hard for them to love me.
the ones i wanted to stay,
i made it so unbearable for them to even wait.

the moment,
i started running out of my breath,
i felt nothing,
but an urge to consume something
to end everything.

so underneath these clothes,
when i reached to cut my heart off,
pull my soul out,
i saw flashbacks of the visions
that i once dreamed of.

"it's not easy to cheat the devil",

this is for the ones
who say
my transformation seems invisble.
everyday i try to take my best shot
with a smile on.
these clothes have been on my skin for ages.
i gave them a name,
but they don't own my soul.
so just hold on,
i'm working on,
and if you don't want to,
that's okay,
i'm still working on.

tomorrow, when you wake up and
look at yourself in the mirror.

please, look at yourself in the mirror.
don't hide, smile.
you may try 10 different outfits,
but when you see in the mirror
wearing them,
look into your eyes,
and don't just stand there.
be a little nicer to yourself today.
i'm sure your soul
carries some dreams,
so whisper to it
that you're still here for them.

my emotions are not unvalid

just because their minds

are on a different trip

everyday

they settle up for the ordinary,
maybe it's meant for them.

but you are extraordinary.

suffering may knock
at your door everyday
but it's your choice to
take it in or
let it stay out

you had been like a drug
that i had been needing.
i had been asking others
for help,
so that i can reach out to you,
and i'd pay anything for that.

but it's been a while,
and i guess
i'm just sober now.

191

somebody told me

if you love someone
you'll be happy to
spend the rest of your
life with them

i'm pretty sure
i could do that with you

You're gonna get everything in your life that you yearn for ...
even if you choose to walk away i'll cherish what you'd leave behind

i'm still teaching myself to be
happy with all that you gave me
and healing myself from
the destiny that couldn't

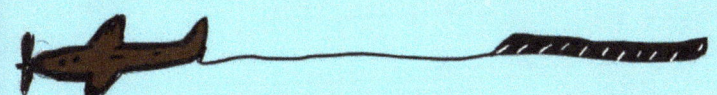

that's okay
i'm learning to let you go
but i hope
we don't become strangers

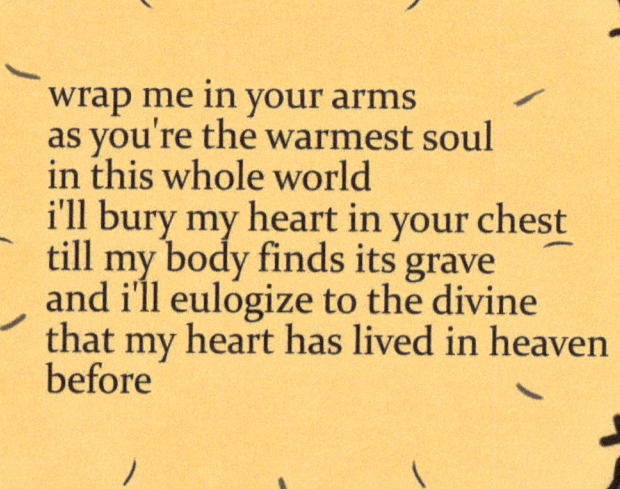

wrap me in your arms
as you're the warmest soul
in this whole world
i'll bury my heart in your chest
till my body finds its grave
and i'll eulogize to the divine
that my heart has lived in heaven
before

i hope you grow flowers out of your chest
that have been concealed within you the whole time

how stupid i was to think
that i ran out of love,
like i'm some sort of wine
that a man consumes every night
before he goes to sleep.
when i'm a daughter
of that mother,
who always taught me to wear my love
all over my soul,
as wisteria
wraps around a tree.
cut me,
i'll grow somehow again.
and i'll grow wildly than ever before,
holding the power
to love in every way,
holding the power
to strangle anything
on the way.

i'll always love you more
and this will be the
only thing between us
that you won't be ever
able to win

i don't wish to be
anyone's responsibility
but someone's dream

...and i wish
to love
selflessly

i've always wanted to
be your favorite
because you've been
mine

loving you
has taught me
what unconditional
means

we all go through the journey of silence
where our words fail to have a voice,
yet i dare your heart to speak.

-k. kanda

THE END

www.ingramcontent.com/pod-product-compliance
Lightning Source LLC
Chambersburg PA
CBHW041114120626
46547CB00019B/2701